SECRET

By EVA KNOX EVANS

A PICCOLO COLOUR BOOK

PAN BOOKS LTD: LONDON

First published in the United States of America 1961 as *Archeology*.
First British edition published 1971 by Pan Books Ltd,
33 Tothill Street, London, S.W.1.

ISBN 0 330 02801 4

Editorial Advisers
Josette Frank, Director for Children's Books,
Child Study Association of America
Dr Leland B. Jacobs, Professor of Education,
Teachers College, Columbia University

Contents

Archaeologists at work

Left, clay tablet of
3,500 years ago

Greek cup (6th century BC)

Below, excavating ancient
Greek palace

Discovering the Past

IT may seem magical that we today know about people who have been dead thousands of years. We know a great deal about where they lived and how they travelled; what they ate and how they cooked. We know about their weapons for hunting and their tools for building.

But it isn't by magic that we know these things. It is the science of archaeology (ar-kee-OL-o-jee) that has made it possible for us to find out so much about the past. The men and women who work in this science are archaeologists (ar-kee-OL-o-jists). They are like detectives who follow clues. They must solve puzzles and clear up mysteries. They must carefully dig deep into the earth because the story of our past is often buried there. Some of them must be deep-sea divers, too. Recent scientific explorations of ancient sunken ships reveal ships built thousands of years ago and the cargo they carried.

How do archaeologists know where to hunt for relics of the past? They don't just take a shovel and begin digging anywhere. That would be a great waste of time. Before they begin, they must come upon some clue that a group of ancient people once lived in a certain spot.

ACCIDENTAL DISCOVERIES

Sometimes a clue is discovered by accident. It could happen this way: a farmer in Germany or France may be ploughing his field when suddenly his plough turns up an object that is strange to him. The farmer might be so curious about it that he would show it to others. He might take it to a nearby university or museum, and finally an archaeologist might get a chance to look at it. Because he has studied ancient relics, the archaeologist might know that this bone or piece of tool had belonged to a group of people who lived thousands of years before. Perhaps more things would be found. The farmer's field might prove to be a good place to dig for ancient treasures.

Some children in America might find a lot of Indian arrow heads in a particular spot where no one believed Indians had

Gold mask **Aztec skull (AD 1324–1521)**

lived. With this clue and careful digging, the archaeologist might find pieces of pottery or stone tools that could fill in more details about some tribe of Indians.

A pilot, flying over a jungle in Central America, might have accidentally spotted a ruin of an old temple. The deep jungle growth had hidden it from sight for many ages past. Or the hunters of chicle, an ingredient in your chewing gum, may have noticed unusual objects. When these reports reached archaeologists, you may be sure they would push through the swampy jungle to explore and dig there.

A great store of pottery, made four hundred years before Christ was born, was found at the bottom of the sea off the coast of southern France. The jars were once cargo on a sunken ship. They were discovered when a deep-sea diver told another diver about a wonderful place to find lobsters.

DETECTIVE WORK

Archaeologists also depend on books to give them clues. Sir Arthur Evans, a famous English archaeologist, studied the legends of the ancient Greeks. Some legends told of a great kingdom on the island of Crete whose capital was Knossos (NOS-us). The remains could not be seen, but Sir Arthur believed the stories might not merely be stories. Perhaps this legendary kingdom was buried.

About sixty years ago, he travelled into the villages and visited the tiny farms of this island in the Mediterranean Sea, looking for clues. He found many of the women wearing curious seals as good-luck charms. They had been picked up on the island, and the inhabitants hadn't the least idea what they were. But Sir Arthur knew. With this clue, he was able to get money for the

A drinking horn shaped like a bull's head was found at Mycenae, Greece

great excavation that revealed the ancient temple of Knossos. Buildings, whole libraries of clay tablets written in a language only recently translated, beautiful art, sculpture and jewellery were found there. So today, we know a great deal about this kingdom and the people who lived there almost four thousand years ago.

Above: engraved cameo dates from the 1st century AD

Right: archaeologists unearthed this Greek statue of Zeus

Vase showing Greek influence

There was a very old church in Vravon near Athens, Greece, that was in need of repair. The Greek Government wanted it to be exactly as it had been 2,500 years ago when it was built. So they got an archaeologist to supervise the job. While he was working on the church, the archaeologist began thinking of stories he had read about Vravon in ancient Greek writings. There were stories about the temples and goddesses; about a priestess who lived near a secret 'holy stairs'; about children dressed as little bears who performed ritual dances to keep away sickness.

These stories had always been thought of as fables. But, thought this Greek archaeologist, suppose some of them were really true? Suppose there was a temple buried under the earth at Vravon?

He and his helpers began to dig. And sure enough, after years of work, the temple and even the secret stairs were found. Since 1948, about six thousand small and beautiful objects have been dug up: mirrors, goblets, rings, vases, statues, all treasures of ages and ages ago.

Ancient people threw out their rubbish just as we do today. When the archaeologist finds these rubbish heaps, he can learn something about the men, women and children who lived so long ago.

In a cave, bones might be found scattered about. Scientists would know what kind of bones they were: reindeer or wild boar, elephant or wolf. If some of the bones were burnt, the archaeologist would know that the people who lived there had learned about fire and liked to eat cooked meat. Needles made of bone have been found, showing that some ancient people wore some sort of clothing. Sharp-pointed spears or arrows tell how the men of an ancient tribe hunted. From knives, fish-hooks and carving tools, we can learn when men discovered the use of iron and other metals. A crude plough blade buried deep in the earth can show where and when people began to stay in one place, and plant and harvest their food.

Tombs and burial grounds tell how people lived in the past. Long ago, many tribes and civilizations believed if they buried a

Thousands worked on the pyramid at Khufu

man with the things he had used in his lifetime, these would help him in his life after death. Tools and pottery, jewellery and works of art were often buried with the dead.

The Egyptians built huge pyramids as tombs for their kings and queens. Great care was taken that every object buried there remained with the dead. The inner rooms of the tombs were sealed and no air reached them. Some wrapped bodies of mummies have been preserved to this day because of

A gold portrait mask of King Tutankhamen and a coffin decorated with paintings and hieroglyphics were found in Egyptian pyramids

the dry climate and the method of embalming the dead developed by the Egyptians.

Archaeologists finally got permission to open these tombs, and knowledge of life thousands of years ago was wonderfully increased. When Howard Carter opened the tomb of King Tutankhamen in 1922, the whole world was excited. For this king was buried with many great treasures.

Two cities at the foot of Mt Vesuvius in Italy were buried completely when the top of that volcano burst apart and lava, mud, fire and water rained down on everything. The cities were Pompeii (pom-PAY-ye) and Herculaneum (her-que-LAN-e-um). This awful tragedy happened on an August morning in the year AD 79. When the sun came out 28 hours later, there was nothing to be seen but a flat ash-covered plain.

Scientists knew these cities had been buried, for there were written records of it. But it was not until 1,700 years later that the engineers and archaeologists began to dig up the cities, buried under as much as 60 feet of lava and earth. It took years of digging to expose them, but there they were as they had been on the summer morning Mt Vesuvius burst apart.

The rows of houses were there with children's toys, cooking pots and scrubbing brushes scattered about inside. The theatres were there and other public buildings. In some places, dishes were still on inn tables, and even coins left by the customers who had hurriedly paid for their meals before

Excavations exposed the ruins of Pompeii

trying to escape the awful lava rain. It was now possible for archaeologists to see how these people lived in the year AD 79.

Clue by clue, scientists have made man's past live again. Because we know something about our ancient ancestors, we can better understand our own life today.

ANCIENT BUILDING STONES

Archaeologists are interested in the building materials of ancient tombs, statues, walls and temples. Why didn't these crumble? To answer this question, archaeologists must study rocks and geology.

Rocks are made of minerals. We can say that the make-up of rocks is similar to the make-up of your favourite fudge, although the two have far different ingredients. When you make chocolate fudge, you mix sugar, cocoa, milk, vanilla and perhaps a pinch of salt. You cook the mixture and then set it aside to harden. It is fudge but it is also a blend of all the things you put into it. In the same way, rocks are a blend of different minerals; sometimes many, sometimes just a few. If you put nuts in your fudge, they would not blend with the sugar, milk and cocoa unless you ground them up first. Sometimes one special mineral doesn't get blended in the rock either and you notice chunks of it, just as you do the nuts in your fudge. The minerals in rocks help us identify them whether they occur as small grains or larger crystals in the ancient building stones.

1. *Limestone or marble.*

These vary in colour, although they are usually grey or white. They may be made of small shells or tiny fused grains that have been built up layer by layer growing around a small nodule or blob. Calcite is the chief mineral in limestone or marble.

2. *Granite.*

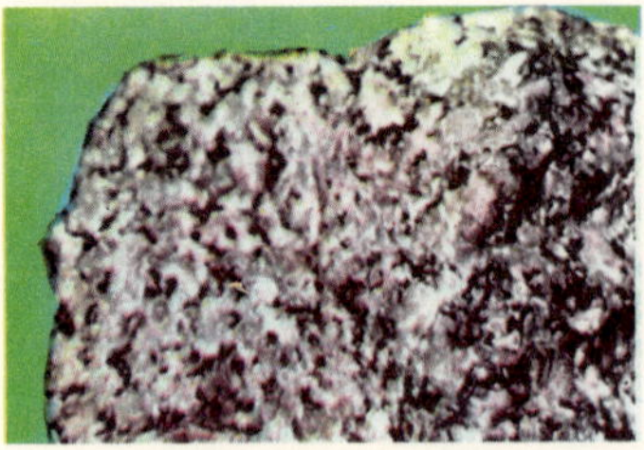

This is a stone of beauty, strength and lasting qualities. It does not weather or crumble easily. How the ancients were able to quarry it in large blocks is a marvel to us.

When you look at granite carefully, you will see tiny rough crystals, almost like bits of broken glass. These are quartz. There may be yellowish grains, with each grain broken into flat shiny surfaces that reflect the light. That is felspar. Between the quartz and felspar you will see dark particles quite different from the other two. These particles, called mica, flake off in thin sheets.

3. *Sandstone.*

This stone is rightly named. The mineral grains of sand have been cemented together by the weight of sediment above them. If the sand grains have been cemented by quartz, the sandstone will be durable enough for a pyramid. If it is lime or iron oxide that fuses the grains, the sandstone will not be as resistant to weather and will crumble.

In ancient Egypt, stones of high quality were available for building. Some regions had good limestone deposits. Near Aswan, where a huge dam has been constructed, there was granite of highest quality. Egyptian civilization was sufficiently advanced for Egyptians to understand the arts of the building trade. With some knowledge and their natural materials, they developed a dignified architecture.

We don't really understand how the Egyptians worked the pink and grey granites. They had little technical 'know-how' or helpful tools. At first, they did not have wheeled vehicles nor the aid of pulleys for lifting things. The muscle power of many men and slaves went into building the great monuments to commemorate their dead kings or rulers. Their feats of engineering in

The Egyptians often inscribed large pillars with hieroglyphics

getting the huge stones out of the earth and into monuments are a source of wonder today.

Suppose a huge slab of granite was desired for an obelisk (OB-e-lisk). This four-sided pillar tapers gradually from the bottom up until it ends in a pyramid at the top. Before the Egyptians could cover the obelisk with hieroglyphic writing to show the world their kings' great feats, the slab had to be cut and removed from the ground.

As we have mentioned previously, granite is not easily quarried. Perhaps they began by cutting a recess or trench in the granite bed. A man in a crouching position could then start the work of quarrying the huge column. When sufficient granite was cut away, there would be room for others to work. To pound, shape and split the stone, they may have used wooden wedges. Much pounding and preparation was necessary to make a surface smooth and regular enough to be inscribed with hieroglyphics. But little by little, the job was done and we are now the beneficiaries since we can read about important events on such a monument.

Workmen carefully unearth an ancient statue of a Roman official

Specialists at Work

THE ARCHAEOLOGICAL TEAM

PIECING together the puzzle of our long-ago ancestors is very difficult. The archaeologist's work is made easier when he can have a team of other scientists to work with him. Assisting the archaeologist in the field, there may be those who are not yet specialized. They work at sifting, digging and sorting.

Let's suppose that one of our universities or museums is sending out a team of scientists to explore a particular area in Spain. It is already known that an ancient tribe once lived on this spot. The problem is to find out more and more about the people who lived there so many years ago. The specialists listed below may accompany the expedition, or, more likely, they will work in laboratories.

An *anthropologist* (an-throw-POL-o-jist) might be needed. This scientist makes a special study of the way people looked, lived and behaved down through the ages to the present time. He would be concerned with the culture or the civilization.

The *palaeontologist* (PAY-lee-un-TOL-o-jist), to whose laboratory unidentified bones are sent, would contribute to the success of the expedition. He is an expert on the animals that lived on this earth from the beginning. He can look at a bone and identify the animal to which it belonged, even though the animal is no longer living on earth. And what is more, he knows when this particular species of animal died out. If the bone was found buried among man-made tools, scientists would know in just what age these people had lived.

A *geologist* (gee-OL-o-jist) makes an important part of the team. He has made a study of the rocks, minerals and earth that make up the crust of the earth. When objects are found in a certain layer of the crust, the geologist may be able to tell when the people who used them lived.

These scientists will need other helpers at their digging site in Spain. For there is much to do.

EXPLORING THE DIGGING SITE

The area can be explored in different ways. It may be divided into sections and numbered. A trench may be dug and the different layers examined. Layers that have accumulated since man occupied this site are of importance to the archaeologists. If walls and floors of structures are found, they are examined carefully. When something is dug up, it is labelled to tell where it was found because its position in the layer is important.

The digging must be done painstakingly so that a precious clay pot or a bone won't be broken by a shovel. Each shovelful of earth must be sifted through a fine wire screen. Often, tiny pieces of an object, no larger than a pin, can give scientists a clue. It would be a great pity if they were accidentally thrown away. Not only shovels are used. Small probes like the ones your dentist uses or a tiny pair of tweezers help dig out important little particles that are embedded in a layer of earth.

Unusual specimens might be carefully packed at the camp site and sent back to the university or museum. There, other archaeologists and scientists have time to study them, determine their age and see how they fit into the puzzle of ancient times. Permission must

Pottery fragments are clues to the archaeologist

be obtained to ship the articles out of the country where the expedition is made. Most governments want to keep the remains of their past.

Important clues to the past are often found in inscriptions on tombs and monuments, on walls of buildings and even on rock faces of mountains and other places difficult to reach. Archaeologists certainly can't take these home with them! But all of these inscriptions must be studied very carefully before they can be deciphered. Often an artist is a part of the archaeological team. His job is to copy the inscriptions as exactly as possible. Photographs help, of course.

Sometimes helpers are hired from the villages nearby. Sometimes students get the exciting chance to go on one of these expeditions and learn while they work.

In Britain keen students, even sometimes children, are allowed to assist in uncovering some relic of the past, such as a Roman villa, or maybe a Viking ship which was left stranded. In Essex, not far from London, some school children helped to remove hundreds of clay pots from a Roman pottery which was active

Sorting chips of pottery is an important task

some 2,000 years ago. At another spot students helped to recover the remains of a mammoth which once roamed the Thames Valley 10,000 years ago.

Modern inventions have been a great help to archaeologists. Earth-moving machines are sometimes used to scrape off the top layer of dirt before the painstaking job of shovelling by hand begins. Reconnaissance planes with their far-seeing cameras can fly over an area and bring back pictures that help the archaeologist plan his work before he travels to the site.

There could be little exploring under-water without the invention of the aqua-lung and all our modern diving equipment.

An underwater archaeologist can now make notes and sketches of an old sunken cargo ship while he is on the ocean floor. Winches and cables, set up on the shore or on a ship, bring specimens up from the deep sea. Television cameras can be set up on the ocean floor so that an archaeologist on the ship or shore can see what is going on below. He can even talk to the skilled divers as they work with their picks and crowbars to separate relics of a ship from stone or coral reefs.

DATING THE FINDS

It is not only important to *find* relics of the past. It is also important to determine how far back into the past they go. The team of scientists who work on an archaeological site can help answer the question: 'How old is it?' The geologist determines the age of the soil in which the objects are found. Inscriptions on temples and monuments often tell who the king was when these structures were built. Once the archaeologist figures out the years of the particular king's reign, the age of the relic can be fixed. Objects that early man used in trading help fix the age of archaeological finds. Coins found among other relics help determine when certain people lived in a particular place. Tree rings also provide clues. Older layers may be compared with newer ones to give a relative date or age.

But how can the archaeologist tell the age of the burnt remains of a camp fire found in a cave in France? How can he know which of the many Indian burial grounds explored in America is the oldest? Until 1948 he couldn't be quite sure. Since then, he has used a wonderful way of finding out about the age of an ancient relic.

The new method of dating, called 'radiocarbon dating', was developed by an atomic scientist, Dr William Libby. This method is based on the presence of radioactive carbon in all organic matter. Scientists had already found out that some of the carbon in carbon dioxide is made radioactive by cosmic rays. Plants take in the carbon dioxide, so they are radioactive, too. And since animals eat plants, some of the radioactive carbon is taken in by them.

Dr Libby found that the concentration of radioactive carbon in any living thing stays the same. The amount taken in is balanced by the amount that decays. When a plant or animal dies, it stops taking in radioactive carbon, and the radioactive carbon already in it continues to decay. The amount of decaying radioactive carbon decreases by half every 5,570 years. So, by measuring the amount of radioactive carbon remaining in the dead plant or animal, Dr Libby could tell how much radioactive carbon it had lost, and how many years had passed since it died and began to lose its radioactive carbon.

Corn can be dated by Dr Libby's method

Sifting a Shovelful of Dirt

If you can find somewhere to dig, in your back yard or garden, or on some waste ground, it would be interesting to see what you can find in a shovelful of dirt. You will probably not find a fossil bone or a cave man's stone cutting-tool. But you may be surprised at what you do discover.

All you will need is:

1. A fine-meshed screen (an old window screen will do).
2. A shovelful of earth.

Put the earth on the screen. Shake the screen gently back and forth until the earth has sifted through. Then carefully examine what is left. Remember that an archaeologist would be interested in a seed, a tiny piece of wood, a chip of broken glass, an old rope, a scrap of cloth.

Making a Cast

At their digging sites, archaeologists sometimes find the imprint of an ancient leaf in a layer of earth, or the footprint of a prehistoric animal embedded in mud that is so old it has turned into stone. They may not be able to remove these clues, so they make plaster casts of them. You can understand how this is done if you make one yourself.

1. Find a good clear animal footprint in some hardened mud. Clear away any sand or sticks with a soft brush.
2. Make a cardboard strip about three inches high and one foot long.
3. Fit the cardboard circle around the footprint and press it into the ground.
4. Pour about $\frac{1}{3}$ cup of water into a pan. Slowly add one cup of plaster of paris to the water.
5. Pour the plaster into the print. It will set in about 20 minutes.

Painting the cast is the finishing touch

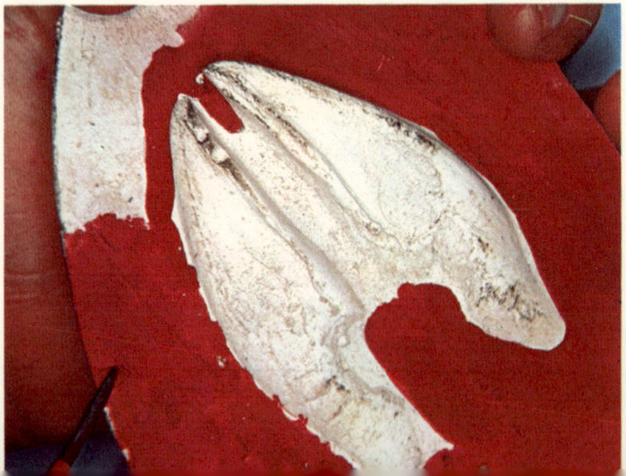

Paintings by cave men were found in the caves of Altamira in northern Spain

The Ancient Artist

CAVE PAINTINGS

THE very early peoples of the world left behind stone, bone and ivory tools and weapons. They left clay pots, baskets and paintings on the walls of caves.

No one knew that cave men were artists until one day about 80 years ago. A four-year-old girl and her father took a walk near their home to explore the Altamira cave in the mountains of northern Spain. This cave was known to have many ancient relics in it and the father hoped to find some.

But his little daughter was bored and she began scrambling over the rocks at the back of the cave. There was a low opening there and when she peered inside she was frightened. She was looking right at the face of a bull! Her father was surprised to discover that the walls and roof of this inner cave were covered with paintings.

No one believed at first that these paintings had been made by cave men. The animals looked so real, the pictures were so beautiful, it just didn't seem possible that people who had lived from 10,000 to 25,000 years ago could paint like that.

But they could. Later, when archaeologists began to look in the back inner rooms of other caves, they found paintings much like the one at Altamira. Drawings, carvings and paintings have also been found in the caves of southwest France, in Italy, and in other places in Spain.

Some of these paintings were coloured with charcoal, ochre and manganese. Little 'paint pots' hollowed out of bone have been found with traces of these colours in them. Engravings were made on stone with stone tools.

When painting cave walls, the cave men must have worked by the light of flares or fires, for no sunlight could have reached those inner rooms.

We hang pictures on our walls to make a room brighter and more interesting; we hang them there so we can look at them all the time. Why were the cave paintings put in places where it was so difficult to see them? Archaeologists believe the paintings may have been used for purposes of magic to make the tribe more lucky in hunting. Some of the animals that were drawn have spears or arrows in them. Perhaps the cave men believed that if a picture were made of a wild boar being killed, the hunters could *really* kill a wild boar more easily.

OTHER EARLY ART

Of course, not everyone lived in caves, so not all of early art was cave drawings. Ornaments whittled out of wood or bone may have been the first kind of art. Each artist used whatever material was around him to express what he wanted to say.

Many Greek statues were found in ancient tombs

In ancient Greece, sculptors made their beautiful statues from the marble that was so plentiful there. In treeless countries covered with ice and snow, seal bones and walrus tusks were used for carving. The Navaho Indians made beautiful sand paintings. The Mayans of Mexico carved their great statues in stone.

There have been artists through the ages in all places of the world. And they have been a great help to archaeologists, for artists have always drawn, painted and carved the things they knew and saw around them. For example, if a picture showed a plough, scientists would know that ploughs were being used at the time the artist painted. When they determine the age of the picture, they know how long ago that kind of plough was used.

Jewels carved out of amber have been found in buried ruins on the Aegean islands near Greece. But amber comes only from the Baltic Sea area near Germany, Norway and Sweden. What do these ancient amber jewels tell the archaeologist? – that there must have been trading thousands of years ago between peoples of these two areas.

In old Egyptian palaces, every room was covered with little paintings showing the way people lived at that time: how they dressed; how they worked their fields and harvested their crops; what their houses looked like. There were even pictures showing the methods they used to clean a fish!

Egyptian artists used 'distemper' – a paint something like whitewash or the wall paints we can buy in a paint or hardware store. They mixed the different colours with a stick glue that dissolved in water. With reed brushes, they painted on walls that were very dry. They had only two colours at first: red and black. But later they discovered how to make yellow, green, blue and dark orange.

Egyptian painting shows workers harvesting grapes

The Magic of the Alphabet

PICTURE-WRITING

OUR ABCs are easy to learn; so easy that we can hardly remember learning them. But it took thousands and thousands of years for the special symbols of the alphabet to be invented. Once, a kind of writing made of pictures called 'pictographs' (PIC-toe-grafs) was used for communication.

We know most about Egyptian pictographs because so many have been found. Egypt is a hot dry country; the climate helped keep the ancient writings from decay. They are especially interesting to us because we know these pictographs are the great-great grandfathers of our own alphabet.

The Egyptians had a lot to write down. Lists of all the valuables in the kings' palaces had to be made. The great and brave deeds of those kings were recorded so that everyone who came after them would know how wonderful they were. At first, the pictographs were cut into wooden or stone tablets. Over the centuries Egyptians discovered how to make paper from the papyrus plant that grew on the banks of the Nile, ink from soot and gum, and pens from sharp-pointed reeds. Using these materials, they could write faster. Their pictures became smaller and gradually the Egyptians began to write in a kind of shorthand.

For example, if they wanted to write the word 'hand', at first they might have drawn a picture of a real hand showing all the five fingers exactly the way a real hand should be. But when they were in a hurry, they wrote it like this: . Gradually that little sign stood for the word 'hand'.

Pictures can tell a story. They can show a man being chased by a tiger, and all of us will know what is happening. But that kind of picture doesn't tell the whole story. It doesn't tell us whether the man was afraid, or out of breath, or near enough to his home to get inside before he was eaten up.

Stories, to be really true, must have some ideas and feelings in them. Early pictographs didn't show that, so the Egyptians began to use their little pictures to show other meanings. This was the pictograph for the word 'eye': . Crying or sadness showed

an eye with tears falling from it; so a picture like this:  began to mean 'sad' or 'weeping'.

A round circle that had just meant 'sun' began now to mean daytime and light. The pictograph for sky was:  . It also began to mean 'heaven'. A star hanging under it not only meant a star in the sky but it could also mean 'night'. This  was the pictograph for mouth. A mouth with lines extended up from it could mean speech or talking.

These pictographs expressed ideas as well as things, so this kind of writing is called 'ideographs' (ID-ee-oh-grafs).

At first, each picture stood for just one thing. But after a while the Egyptians began

Ideographs of horses and donkeys, and the numerals 2, 3, 4 and 5 are inscribed on this tablet

Egyptians carved pictographs on wood panels

to put two or three pictures together to represent a specific object, like a water jug.

But the Egyptians didn't stop there. They kept on learning new things and, as they did, they needed new ways to write them down. Gradually, through the ages, some of the pictographs began to stand for sounds of words instead of for ideas or just the thing itself. These pictures are called 'phonograms' (FONE-o-grams) because 'phono' means sound.

The idea of using pictures for the sounds of words or syllables was a very exciting thing to happen. It took several thousand years of writing with pictographs and ideographs before someone thought of doing it.

Once ideographs and phonograms were thought of, writers didn't stop using pictographs. They now had three different ways to write down their stories and thoughts: pictographs, ideographs, and phonograms.

Before the invention of phonograms, writing and reading had nothing to do with speaking. We must learn a language before we can write it down or read it. The pictographs of the ancient Egyptians could be read by people who didn't know the Egyptian language. For a picture of a fish always meant a fish, no matter what language you used to say the word.

If we were using pictographs, a picture of a cat would mean cat whether we were French and called it 'chat', or German and called it 'katz'.

It takes a kind of artist to write this way and not all of us are that talented. Nor were all the Egyptians, and as more and more people learned to write, the pictures changed. For instance, in the beginning this was a pictograph for 'door'  and doors in those times may have looked like that. Then, because that pictograph took a long time to write, the word 'door' was written this way:  and finally it was made like this,  which you can see is a much quicker way of writing it.

As ages went by, the pictures became so simple that they looked like a curious kind of alphabet. But the Egyptians never entirely gave up their little pictures. Maybe they thought the pictures were pretty and decorated their pages. They may have needed them to explain the meanings of words. Our word today for all three kinds of Egyptian picture-writing is 'hieroglyphics' (HY-er-o-GLYF-ix).

Egyptians were not the only people who thought of writing things down. In Babylonia,

This Sumerian tablet shows their cuneiform writing

people were writing at about the same time or even earlier. But the Babylonians had no papyrus plant for making paper and no reeds for pens. They wrote on clay with a sharp-pointed stick or 'stylus'.

It was hard to push or pull the stylus through the wet clay. So Babylonians did not write with pictographs. Instead, they made wedge-shaped forms by pushing the stylus point into the clay, then pressing down with a sharp side of the stylus. Their writing looked very different from the Egyptians' although they had some of the same ideas for their pictographs. The Egyptians used this symbol  for *sun*. But the Babylonians made it this way: . Just as in our valentines today,  is the symbol for a heart in many of the old, old pictographs wherever they are found all over the world. But not in Babylonia. This is the way they wrote it:  . And all because it was easier when they were pushing a stylus through wet clay.

This kind of writing is called 'cuneiform' (ku-NE-i-form) because 'cuneus' is the Latin word for wedge. Archaeologists have found

The Babylonians wrote letters in cuneiform on biscuits of clay

many examples of cuneiform writing in their excavations, for not only the Babylonians used it. This wedge-shaped writing changed and became simplified until it too began to look something like an alphabet.

THE DEVELOPMENT OF THE ALPHABET

The Ancient Egyptians stayed home and figured things out for themselves. But they had neighbours who went places. About three thousand years ago, the Phoenicians, living on the east coast of the Mediterranean Sea, began to build boats and travel about. And because they did, they began to develop the ABCs that we use today.

The Phoenicians were farmers, craftsmen and manufacturers. They were also traders, buying what some had to sell and taking it to sell to others who needed it. They needed writing for their business dealings. They didn't bother with pictures at all. No one knows just where they got their alphabet. They may have picked it up from many different peoples, although we are quite sure they got many letter symbols from the Egyptians.

In travelling about, the Phoenicians learned about papyrus which they bought and sold. It was the only paper known then and the easiest thing to write on. They learned how to write on it and invented nineteen letters but none of these were vowels.

As you know, a, e, i, o, u, and sometimes y, are the vowels in our alphabet. The rest of the letters are consonants. We would have a hard time writing words without both kinds, but this didn't seem to bother the Phoenicians.

W hp sh lks ths bk – that's the way the Phoenicians would have written 'We hope she likes this book'. It wouldn't be the easiest

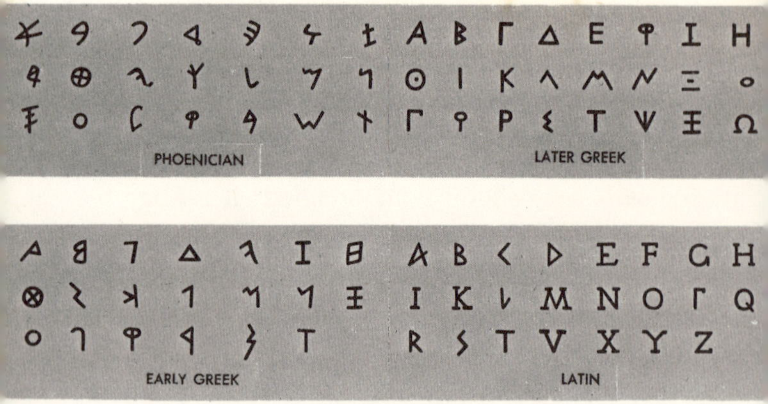

The Phoenician alphabet was adapted by the Greeks and later by the Romans

writing to read, for it would take someone good at puzzles to figure it out. But about all the Phoenicians ever wrote were lists of things they were buying and selling. 'Pprs' would have stood for papyrus; 'gm' for gum; and 'shlls' for shells. It is very much the way we write GB for Great Britain.

When the Greeks got hold of this alphabet, they added vowels, thus changing it to suit their needs. They liked to write stories, plays and long poems. They turned some of the consonants which the Phoenicians had invented into vowels, and added new letters of their own until they had twenty-four.

The Romans got their alphabet from the Greeks and they changed some of the letters, too. Because our language comes straight from the Latin or Roman language, we use the same letters the Romans used more than 2,000 years ago.

THINGS TO DO

Making a Stylus

A stylus made of sharpened stone, bone or wood was the 'pen' used for writing in clay. You can make one by sharpening the end of a stick or, better still, a cane. Cut a piece about six inches long. It can be sharpened in a regular pencil sharpener.

If you use your stylus to write in clay, you may need to resharpen it when you use it with ink.

Making a Clay or Plaster Tablet

At the dawn of history, tablets were made from the clay soil that the ancients found around them. If clay soil is not available, you can do some interesting experiments

with powdered clay or with plaster of paris.

You will need a mould to make a clay tablet. An aluminium-foil pan, greased lightly, can be used to make a plaster tablet, or you can use a small cardboard box, lined with waxed paper.

Mix the plaster of paris according to instructions on the package. Pour the mixture into the mould to a depth of about $\frac{1}{4}$ inch. Tap the sides lightly to get out any air bubbles. After about 10 minutes press the mixture lightly with your finger. If it seems set, it is time to get out your stylus and write on the tablet. Work quickly, for the tablet will dry in about 20 minutes. When the tablet has set, remove from the mould.

Making Ink

The ancients used many materials to make their ink. The main thing was to make the ink a different colour from the paper they used. Soot was an important ingredient in black ink; ochre was used for red. Plants and berries were used, too. Often the ink was dried into little hard cakes and moistened when it was needed.

Experiment with making ink from flower petals. You will need:

1. Red, blue or purple petals from roses, zinnias, poppies or cornflowers, for instance. The red ones are best, but you can mix the colours if you don't have enough of one kind.
2. A little clean sand.
3. Soluble alcohol.

Cut up the petals into an old cup until it is about half-full. Add a teaspoon of sand. Pour in soluble alcohol to cover.

This mixture must be ground fine in order to get all of the colour from the petals. An empty pop bottle will do for the pestle or grinder. Set aside for about an hour. Then strain the ink into another cup or bottle.

Cuneiform and hieroglyphic signs on this seal make it the first bilingual text ever found

The Written Word

SCRIBES; SCROLLS AND CLAY TABLETS

IN ancient times, people who knew how to write were very important indeed. Only a few special people could do it. They were called 'scribes'. Mighty kings and emperors, who couldn't read or write themselves, had their own scribes and these men were almost as important as their rulers.

If they were writing on papyrus, scribes sat on the floor at a low writing bench. Slaves fanned the flies away and poured cool water over the scribe if he got too hot. Nothing at all was allowed to disturb this wonderful man who knew how to write.

As we know, writing developed in different parts of the world. Much of this writing has been lost because it was written on materials that didn't last through the thousands of years until archaeologists could find it. Often, too, people didn't think it was important to keep what they had written, just as we today tear up letters and put them in the wastebasket or throw newspapers and magazines into the dustbin.

But fortunately for us, many early writings were so carefully stored, they could be found ages after they were written. Thus, we know about ancient alphabets and what people were writing thousands of years ago. The scribes were important while they were alive and writing, and they are also important to us today.

The Egyptians and Babylonians used writing a lot. The Egyptians could use papyrus, so they were able to invent something else: the rolled book, or scroll. With papyrus, no matter how long the text, it could be put together on one long roll and read like a book. These scrolls were wound around sticks, tied with papyrus tape, and often sealed with a special seal made of mud from the banks of the Nile. Then the rolls

The illustrations in the Egyptian Book of the Dead were painted on papyrus

were stored in hollowed-out wood containers. Parchment made from the skins of sheep or goats was also used for rolls.

As you know, the Babylonians did not have papyrus and they used stone or clay for their writing material. Long texts required many tablets. In order to make sure that one 'page' would follow the next in proper order the scribes would write the first line of the next tablet at the bottom of the preceding one. This helped keep them from getting mixed up. For the same reason, we number our pages when we are writing a long composition.

ANCIENT LIBRARIES

Because these tablets were so hard to keep together, the Babylonians made special places to store them. They were probably the ones who really invented the library.

About 75 years ago, archaeologists from the University of Pennsylvania discovered a huge library in Nippur, the oldest city of ancient Babylon. Many tablets found there were of unbaked clay and were not as well preserved as others. But there were enough tablets found to tell us much about these early people.

The tablets were stored on shelves about 18 inches wide. This library was connected to a great temple. There had also been a school in the temple, for among the ruins were many texts that had been prepared by teachers. There were also tablets of exercises written by the students. It was important that a scribe teach others how to write, so there would be scribes to take his place when he died.

There was an enormous library in ancient Alexandria, Egypt, thought to have contained 700,000 rolls or books. This city was an important port and was invaded over and over again. One invader ordered the library burned and most of the precious rolls of papyrus were lost in the fire.

In 1947, another ancient library was discovered. Two Arab shepherds who lived on the rocky coast of the Dead Sea in Palestine were looking for a goat which had wandered from the fold. Rising from the Dead Sea coast are great cliffs, and scattered among the cliffs are small caves. About 400 feet up one of these cliffs, the shepherds found an opening and one of them threw a stone in to see if he could frighten the goat out of hiding.

Instead of the goat's bleat, they heard the clatter of broken pottery. They crawled inside. In the dim light, they saw several tall straight-sided jars with upside-down bowls for covers. When the shepherds took off these lids, they were disappointed to find only old rolls of brittle leather or parchment covered with writing.

The Dead Sea Scrolls were found in jars similar to these Cretan ones

But they took several of the rolls back to their tent village to show what they had found. A friend suggested they might be able to get money for the rolls if they took them to the nearest town, Bethlehem. By roundabout ways, these ancient rolls were finally examined by archaeologists, who knew they were valuable. In the neighbourhood of the first cave were nine other caves, containing many more jars filled with rolls written in old Hebrew script. These discoveries were called the Dead Sea Scrolls, and they might never have been found if a frisky little goat had not run away.

PROFESSIONAL LETTER-WRITERS

While many of the early scribes wrote only for the libraries of their kings or for their temples, others were involved in all kinds of business deals. Scribes were needed to write lists of cargo for trading ships, or letters to whoever was getting a shipment. Lists of household goods and accounts of food supplies on hand in the great palaces were made. In Mexico, both the Aztecs and the Mayans made books of deerskin. One

The scribes were men who could read and write. They held positions of responsibility in ancient kingdoms

ruler had a whole house full of these books just for his kitchen accounts.

In Old Testament times, professional letter-writers used to sit at the gates of the cities looking for someone who would pay them to write a letter. They carried papyrus rolls, or wooden forms with wax poured in them; a stylus or reed pens, and cakes of ink – both red and black. As soon as someone came along who needed something written, the letter-writer ground off some ink with a stone, moistened it with water and wrote down the message.

Business men today have secretaries who type their letters for them, and the business man signs his name at the bottom. But in those times, the business man didn't know how to write his name. He carried a seal tied to a string around his neck. When the scribe had finished the letter, the man signed his name to it by pressing his seal into the wax tablet or a drop of wax on the papyrus.

A man's seal was a very important thing. They were carved out of stone or bone; or metal after metals were discovered. Each

Two seals show tumblers performing handstands and an acrobat somersaulting over a bull

man had his own special design. Some seals belonging to kings and rulers were beautifully and elaborately carved. Others were just crude marks, but once they were pressed into clay or wax, they showed which man owned what, whether it was a clay jar, a bale, a box or a letter.

THINGS TO DO

Making a Seal

A seal can be made of almost any hard material that can be pressed into wax. The important thing is that you work out your own design so the seal will be especially yours. You could carve your initials or a pictograph, or carve a drawing of your favourite pet.

The seal can be made in various ways:

1. Carve a design on one side of a small block of wood or linoleum, or
2. Use about 2 inches of ordinary modelling clay and shape it into a cube. Make your design on one side before the clay has hardened completely, or
3. Pour a little plaster-of-paris mix into a very small paper cup. Tap the sides

gently to get out the bubbles. When it is firm, make your design, but let it harden completely before you remove it from the paper-cup mould.

4. Use melted candle wax, paraffin wax or regular sealing wax from a stationery shop to make an impression of your seal.

Making a Wax Tablet

The children who went to the early Roman and Greek schools used wax tablets to write their alphabet and numbers on. These were simply wooden forms with rims high enough to hold a layer of wax. These tablets could be used over and over again, because when the wax was melted, the letters or figures were 'erased'. Then the wax would harden again into a smooth tablet.

With a cake of paraffin or a melted candle you can make a tablet, too. A square or rectangular aluminium-foil pan (frozen foods are often packed in these) can be used for the wax tablet form. Put a cake of paraffin into one of these pans and set it in a *warm* oven. The wax will melt into an even 'page'. When it hardens, write on it with a stylus.

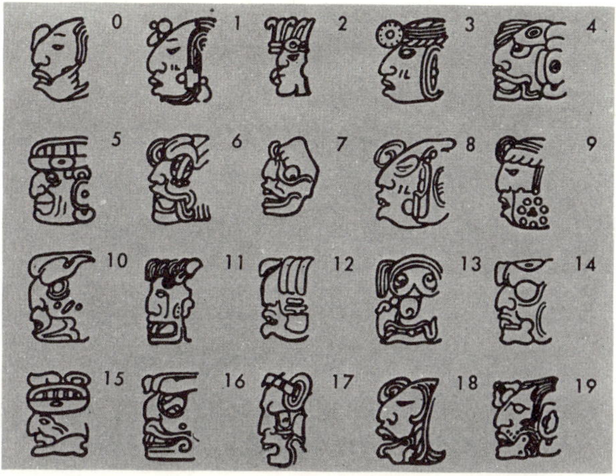

Early Mayan numbers were written in hieroglyphics on paper made from fig-tree fibres

The Magic of Numbers and the Marking of Time

ARCHAEOLOGISTS have helped construct the history of arithmetic. Arithmetic probably began before writing or reading, and developed from man's awareness of numbers. He understood the meaning of 2, although he probably couldn't count and he certainly couldn't write the number down. But he knew about that number because he had 2 eyes, 2 ears, 2 hands and 2 feet.

Then came the number 5. You know why: 5 fingers on each hand, 5 toes on each foot. If 5 weren't enough he could use 10 because man can count the fingers on both hands. What about 20? That was just as easy. Count all your fingers and all your toes and you know what you get.

Ten was, and still is, the most often-used number base. It probably became the basis for counting because it is so easy to count on the fingers. The American Indians, though, used 5 as their number base, and the Mayan Indians of Mexico used 20.

COUNTING DEVICES

But 2, 5, 10 and 20 weren't enough numbers to know. For example, the chief of a tribe had to know how many men were in his tribe so he would know how many he could depend on if he went to war. He had to count them, and even if his tribe was very small, there might be more men than the number of his fingers and toes. If a man had sheep or goats, he wanted to know how many he had so he would know whether any of them were lost or stolen.

To count the people in his tribe, the chief may have used one twig for each person. In some places, twigs might not have been handy. So pebbles, shells or notches on a stick helped people to count. One of the earliest counting devices was a knotted rope or leather thong. One knot probably stood for 10 people or 10 goats. The knots were counted and multiplied by 10 to get the total number. The Incas of Peru used knotted cords for counting. Sometimes these were hung from a wooden crossbar with the cords dyed different colours to represent different numbers. To this day, shepherds in the high mountains of Peru count their sheep in this way.

From left to right, the knots stand for the numbers from 1 to 9

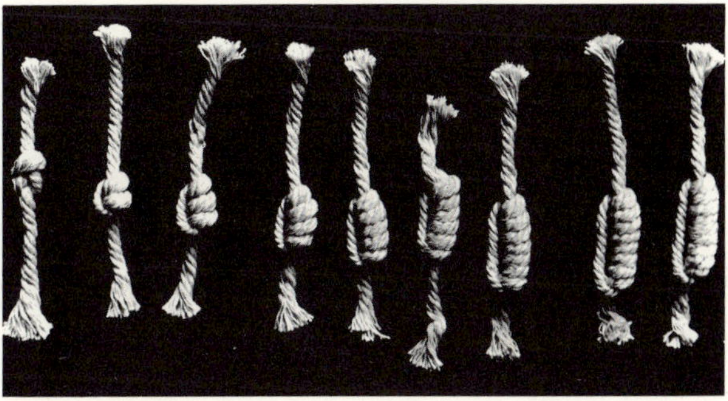

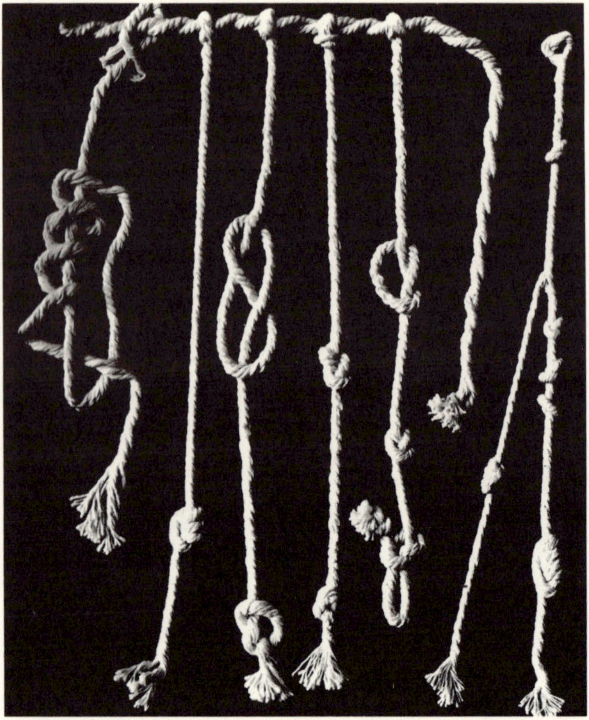

Different knots had different meanings

This knotted cord is called a 'quipu' (KE-poo). It was not only used for counting and recording numbers, but also for communicating. A messenger who knew exactly what each knot and coloured cord stood for could convey the message to the person he was sent to see.

Suppose a warrior king of ancient Persia decided to take his armies and invade another country. He may have left behind a group of soldiers to guard an important bridge – and he wanted that bridge guarded for exactly sixty days.

Today he would have told his captain: 'Stay by this bridge from September 9th to November 8th, and then if I have not returned, you may leave'.

But the ancient king couldn't do that because he had no calendar. Instead he took a long leather quipu and tied sixty knots in it. The captain of his guard was instructed to untie one knot each day and when all the knots were untied, their guard duty was over. Then, too, a messenger sent on a trip carried a quipu to tell him how long he had been away and when he should return.

Multiplication, addition, subtraction and division were used, although not named as such. In most early tribes, food was shared by all. To share equally, they had to divide. And if the headman of a tribe wanted to find out how much food would be left over for another day, he had to subtract.

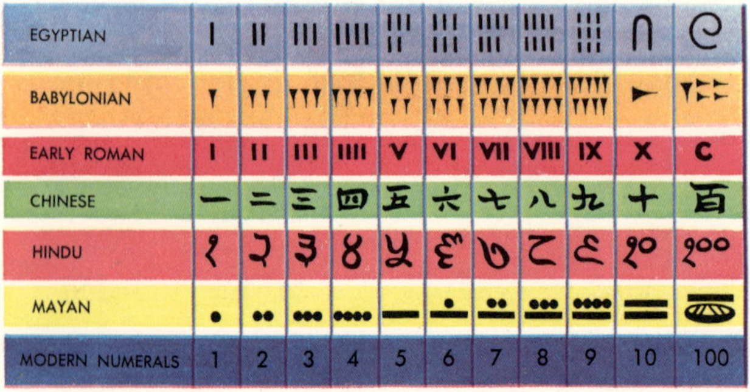

Early peoples developed different number systems

WRITTEN ARITHMETIC

The Egyptian kings who were very rich had special men to do their counting for them. Their great monuments, the Pyramids and the Sphinx, required complicated arithmetic in planning and building. The architects used two fractions, $\frac{2}{3}$ and $\frac{3}{4}$, to show what was left when one part of three was taken away from three; and when one part of four was taken from four.

The Romans wrote their numbers one to ten in this way: I, II, III, IV, V, VI, VII, VIII, IX, X. There was no zero in this system and the cumbersome letters made higher mathematics difficult. There were only seven symbols: I for 1; V for 5; X for 10; L for 50; C for 100; and M for 1,000. This was possible because they used both addition and subtraction in working out a system for their numbers. As you know, an I in front of V means that you take one away from five leaving four. Put the I after the V and add to make six. An X stands for 10; put three of them in a line – XXX, and you have 30. An X before L(50) means 40 because you are subtracting 10. And with an X after L, you are adding 10 to 50, which would make 60.

You may have had fun writing notes in code by using numbers instead of letters. 'Dear Joe' would be written: 4-5-1-18 10-15-5. The ancient Greeks did the opposite and used their alphabet for numbers. Of course, this could have been confusing. How would you know whether someone was writing letters or numbers? The Greeks took care of that by putting an accent mark to the right of each letter when it was being used as a number.

The Western system of writing numbers is called 'Arabic' because the Arabs introduced it into Europe, and it came to America from there. The numerals for each number are the same, but the words are in the different languages.

All peoples down through the ages have needed to know about numbers. They had to count and figure or they couldn't have built monuments or ships. Numbers helped people figure out measures of land, grain and money and also the seasons, the days, years, and the time of day.

An AD 1564 water clock measured hours as water drained from a counterweighted bucket

Making a Quipu

You can make a counting rope or quipu very easily.

1. Take a soft rope about three feet long.
2. Tie a knot at each end and dip the knots in a little paraffin, or candle, wax. This will keep the rope from unravelling.
3. Then tie knots along the rope at equal distances apart. You will be the one to decide whether each knot stands for 5, 10, 50 or 100.
4. If you want the knots on the same rope to stand for several different numbers, they can be spaced in various ways. You might try double knots for certain numbers and single knots for others.
5. A more complicated quipu can be made by using several shorter ropes. These should be tied to the main counting rope so that they hang down from it. You might use heavy wool or cotton threads in different colours. Then the colours would show the different amounts each knot stands for.

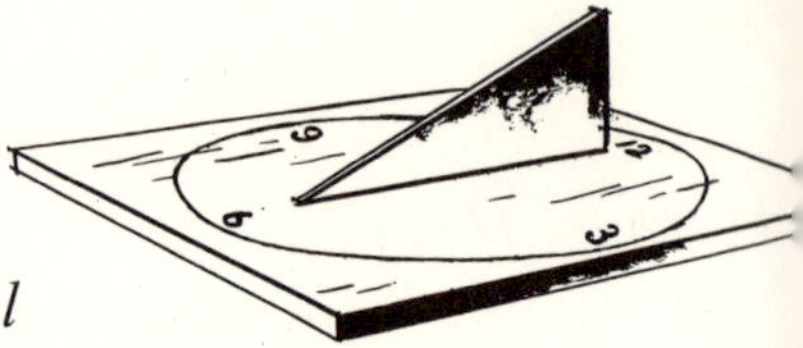

Making a Sundial

A common ancient time keeper was the sundial which marked hours, half-hours and even quarter-hours. You can make one.

Measure and cut a piece of wood or tin into a two-foot square. Mark the hours on your square just as they are on a clock face. Your dial will look like a square handless clock. Now you will need something to cast a shadow. Most sundials have a right-angled triangle for this. It is called a 'gnomon' (NOH-mon). Make one about one foot long out of wood or metal. The picture will show you how to place the gnomon on the dial. Notice that the right angle of the triangle is at 12 o'clock and the apex is at 6. Fasten the gnomon to the dial.

Ancient Greeks and Romans used sundials to tell time

Place the dial in a position where sunlight will fall on it. If your own clock says 11 o'clock, turn your sundial until the shadow from the gnomon falls on the number 11. Leave your sundial in that spot and it will keep time. (Remember, the sun pays no attention to daylight saving time.)

Making a Candle Clock

Measure a straight-sided candle. Let's suppose it is four inches long. Set it in a holder and light the wick. Notice the exact time on your watch or clock. When 15 minutes have passed, blow out the candle.

Measure the candle again to see how much shorter it is. The difference between the two measurements will show how much of the candle burned in 15 minutes. Suppose $\frac{1}{2}$ inch has burned. Measure $\frac{1}{2}$ inch from the top of the candle and mark with a line scraped into the wax. Then mark $\frac{1}{2}$ inch from that line and so on down to the bottom of the candle. You will have a clock that measures quarter-hours.

Any experiment involving fire must be done with care.

The Translators

FINDING THE KEY TO CUNEIFORM WRITING

WHEN the clay tablets with their strange cuneiform writing, and the papyrus rolls with their hieroglyphics were first found, no one could read them. Scientists worked many years, but they did not solve the puzzles. They were finally solved by two people: a German school teacher, and the son of a French librarian, who found the keys.

Georg Grotefend was born in Germany in 1775. His father was a cobbler. Georg was determined to get an education and he did. He eventually became the vice-principal of a grammar school in Frankfurt. When he was 27 years old, he believed he could decipher cuneiform writing, and at a party one night he bet his friends that he could.

Many of the people who had tried to translate the ancient writings were students of old languages, but Grotefend was not. He was a man who loved to solve puzzles and codes. The only samples of cuneiform writing that Georg had were some bad copies of a few inscriptions from ancient monuments of Persia.

Grotefend didn't know whether the writing read from left to right, or right to left; down and up, or up and down. But as he studied the writing, he discovered two things:

1. One group of signs appeared over and over again.
2. One diagonal wedge also appeared frequently.

Georg decided the group of signs which appeared most frequently must stand for the word 'king'. He knew that in ancient times kings were the only ones who had monuments built. He also knew that most monuments to kings gave lists of their ancestors: King So and So, son of King So and So, and on down the line.

The diagonal wedge, he decided, was used to separate one word from the next and wasn't a letter at all. This was the beginning of Grotefend's key to the puzzle. It took a lot more work, of course, before he was able to decipher the writing and translate the marks into an alphabet. The names of the kings who belonged to the monuments were known. so Grotefend was able to see which wedges stood for the sounds in those names.

In this way, he was able to decipher more and more cuneiform letters until he had the sounds that matched each wedge.

FINDING THE KEY TO HIEROGLYPHICS

It was twenty years later that Jean-Francois Champollion, the Frenchman, found the key to ancient Egyptian writing. At the age of 12, he first saw a papyrus with the strange hieroglyphics. He asked if anyone could read them. When he was told no one could, he said that some day he was going to do it. He did decipher the hieroglyphics and it happened this way.

When Napoleon's armies invaded Egypt, one of his soldiers dug up a large flat stone. It was black, about the size of a table top, and covered with writing. It was called the Rosetta Stone because it was found near a town of that name.

Champollion saw a copy of the Rosetta Stone. It was written on in three different ways. One of the ways was hieroglyphics, another was demotic (de-MOT-ick) script, which was a quick way of making pictographs. And the third was Greek.

The Greek was easy for Champollion to read and he learned that the tablet was about the Egyptian king, Ptolemy (TOL-e-mee). Since he also knew a lot of the ancient languages, he knew that in Egyptian, the name is spelled 'Ptolmis'.

One group of hieroglyphics was surrounded by an oval, called a 'cartouche' (car-TOOSH). This was the only group of signs that had a cartouche around it, so Jean-Francois decided it stood for the name of the king, Ptolemy. It was one key to the puzzle, but

The hieroglyphics on the Rosetta Stone were a puzzle to scientists for many years

he needed more proof to be sure. He found the proof when another inscription

Ptolemy

was uncovered that was written in both hieroglyphics and Greek. This one was about Cleopatra. And again a group of signs were enclosed in a cartouche. Now he could compare the two because some of the same signs appeared in both.

Cleopatra

Of course, Champollion didn't stop there. He collected more of the inscriptions and learned more of the ancient symbols of the Egyptian hieroglyphics. He finally had a list of all the symbols.

Because of Grotefend, Champollion and many others like them, it is possible for students today to learn to read the ancient writings. But translating them is still very hard. When archaeologists find clay tablets or papyrus rolls, they are not always in one piece. Clay tablets get broken, papyrus falls to pieces, leather scrolls become brittle and chip and break. Sometimes these writings are found by people who don't realize how important they are, so they are handled carelessly and parts get lost.

Archaeologists have to piece these together like giant jigsaw puzzles. Sometimes the pieces are no bigger than fingernails. Often one 'page' of a clay tablet is bought by a museum in England and the page that follows it is owned by a museum in Turkey. Reading a book that way is very hard.

There is still much to be found out about ancient languages and alphabets. The hieroglyphics of the Etruscans who lived in Italy long before the Romans have not been deciphered. Seals found in the Indus Valley of northwest India are covered with curious pictographs whose meanings remain a mystery. The origin of the Easter Island pictographs is still an enigma. Only in the last ten years or so, Michael Ventris, a young Englishman, found a way to decipher the tablets uncovered at Knossos. Some day all of the mysteries will be solved. You may even have a part in solving them!

INDEX

** Illustration only*

Credits: Agora Museum, Athens, Greece: 22, 25; American Museum of Natural History: 65, 66; Archaeological Museum in Herakleion: 9; *Ancient Rome*, © copyright 1964 by The Odyssey Press: 10 (top); Arizona State Museum: 4 (top), 27, 30; Art Reference Bureau: 4 (middle right); Ashmolean Museum, Oxford: 52, 60; Black Star: 16; British Museum: 7 (right), 14 (right), 54; Dr Alfonso Caso: 7 (left); Wilson and MacPherson Hole: 46; Metropolitan Museum of Art: title page; Museum of Fine Arts, Boston: contents page; Sheik Abd el Qurna: 38; *Picture History of Archaeology*, published by Thames and Hudson, Ltd: 10 (right); Roy Pinney: 32; Toledo Museum of Art: 10 (right); J. W. Watson: 4 (bottom), 20.

Drawings: Campbell Grant: 4 (middle left), 33, 41; Lowell Hess: 50; Harry McNaught: 70, 72 (bottom).